THE ISLANDERS

PHILIP BOOTH

The

Islanders

1961

THE VIKING PRESS

New York

First published in 1961
by The Viking Press, Inc.
625 Madison Avenue, New York 22, N.Y.

Published simultaneously in Canada
by The Macmillan Company of Canada Limited

Library of Congress catalog card number:
61-17222

Printed in the U.S.A.
by Vail-Ballou Press, Inc.

THANKS

to the editors of the following magazines

Audience

Chelsea

The Chicago Review

Furioso

Harper's

The Hudson Review

The Kenyon Review

The London Magazine

The New Yorker

The Paris Review

Poetry

Saturday Review

The Virginia Quarterly Review

Voices

in which poems contained in the present collection were first published

and to

The John Simon Guggenheim Memorial Foundation

which made possible

the best part

of

this book

For
My Father

Contents

I

II

III

10

THE ISLANDERS

The question that he frames in all but words
Is what to make of a diminished thing.
—ROBERT FROST

I

THE SECOND NOON

New to light that first noon,
they stand blind in the sun's meridian,
and own no sight, but hang their heads down
from that glare and first heat
until, as the day grows cool,
their accustomed eyes can open,
and they recognize the original shadows
leaning out from their feet.

Asking that afternoon nothing,
they worship those doubled forms who swim
before them onto the streaming meadows.
Grown tall at last to turn
questions, they face behind them,
full West, and—stumbling blind
beyond guesses of dawn—are pressed
into the aggregate shadows.

They wake to a slivered moon
that first night, to a sky wet with stars,
and in that world cannot believe
they see. And will not see
(as light from love revolves)
until, as their shadows come home
foot by foot, they learn to look not to the sun,
but full, at high noon, to themselves.

THE COUNTERSHADOW

In daylight, even,
walking that same
suburban street
I take back home
at night, I mind
how I repeat
myself, past lamp-
posts, drunken with
the countershadow
that I drag, feet-
first, closing on
my heels until,
within the arc
beside me, I
surpass myself,
to lunge across
the curb and, two-
lengths tall, race
leaning up the
laddered squares,
as if to chart
some progress, or
intent, that half-
way to the public
light, dissolves
in dark cement.

CONVOY

One blueberry morning in Maine,
turned home with a full quart pail
in the bilge, I saw a dog seal
on a ledge across from Castine.

In the flooding tide, like a rock
awash on that shoal ridge,
the seal lay stretched on warm ledge,
sunning until my struck oarlock

warned him awake. Aloof
yet inquisitive, he at first arched
his trick back and then as I watched
him upwind, flipped, and slid off.

I ate a berry, sure
he'd surface to see what fool
creature I was. No seal.
Then by my leeward oar

his wet dog head slid up.
I saw a salt drop drip
off his whiskers and *plop,*
he was gone. He was fed up

with man, I thought. I was wrong:
he came up to try the port side,
silver-brown, eyes still wide.
An expanding silver ring

of millpond framed him, but beneath
that mirror I could not see.

I looked at him. He
regarded me. Then with deep breath

he dove as if under my skiff,
and I heard a new breath drift
downwind. Only a ring was left
when I looked; my neck was stiff

with watching, I'd turned too slow,
and as my mind encompassed
such double luck, I focused
on my error. His alter ego

or twin had submerged to explore.
Only one seal or his true love
surfaced in corners of
my sight, for a full half-hour.

I never saw both; the sport
was submarine: when a starboard
nose broke water, then, with a hard
seal slap, a tail submerged to port.

That was my convoy home: a seal
splash (not caught crab or riptide)
rippling one or the other side.
At least one seal was real.

And I, least wise in Maine,
with double delight and half dread
flooding two good eyes and one head,
rowed home on my single plane.

WAS A MAN

Was a man, was a two-
faced man, pretended
he wasn't who he was,
who, in a men's room,
faced his hung-over
face in a mirror hung
over the towel rack.
The mirror was cracked.
Shaving close in that
looking glass, he nicked
his throat, bled blue
blood, grabbed a new
towel to patch the wrong
scratch, knocked off
the mirror and, facing
himself, almost intact,
in final terror hung
the wrong face back.

MORES

On the phone they said
Come as you are. So I
came, though my costume was weird

for their masquerade
picnic, came naturally
as a barefoot man with a beard.

Some chose to wrestle
in masks, others outdrank
their wives or they played old games

like King of the Castle.
I sat apart on a rock,
matching their masks to known names

and marveling how they
all were well gotten up,
until one came to recognize

my face, and the party
danced to a sudden stop.
I, he announced, had won the prize

as Most Original.
But when I would not strip
my beard at his soft direction,

then these congenial
people lifted me up,
and played at a small crucifixion.

SPIT

In memory of Arthur Moffatt,
a Conscientious Objector, who
froze to death September 14, 1955,
exploring the Canadian Barren Grounds.

The Chipewyans play it.
They used to hunt,
or lug in white
man's radar. They
hunt Under-
the-Blanket now,
make hot thunder
in big snow
and, melted, wait
for Treaty Day:
the solstice when
the Government
lands, with cash.
Squaws and Indians
crowd up. *Don't,*
the priest explains.
He talks Chipewyan
like a white man.
He says *wash,*
and how, until
ice-out, God won't
pay off again.
Any Christian Indian
knows that. They wait
the end of Treaty
Day, then play
the old game, Spit:
first squaw chooses
first man, that first

man stands still.
Next man spits
on first man's chest:
spit runs right
or left, he loses;
if spit hits
his navel, wins.
The Chipewyans
play it. The laws
are old: when light
and cash run out,
they play for squaws.
Far into arctic
midnight, thick
with phlegm, they bet
on this old game
new civilizations
have no name
for. Only nations
like the Chipewyans
play it. Spit
is what they call it.
Spit.   Spit.   Spit.

THE TOWER

Strangers ask,
always, how tall
it is. Taller,
the natives say,
than any other.
Watching it sway,
slightly, in a brisk
wind, you believe
them and feel,
well, smaller
than you once
did, or would have,
even had they woken
somebody's father,
who remembers
every specification,
they say, having fought
against this location,
in the last elections
before it was built.
It is enough
to see it, canted
over you, as
you approach
the strange base:
a cement stilt
set in a rough
patch of marsh;
on that, a ball
with numbers
etched on it,
perhaps a date,

on which the steel
frame, in one
brave unbroken
line, seems to stretch
for heaven itself,
in three diminishing
sections. The balance
is fantastic,
or seems so, until
you recall the elastic
web of guy wires
that, slanted
beyond you, support
the tower in nine
equal directions.
The local women,
hanging their wash
on a wet line,
Monday, report
that it's hidden
in clouds, out
of mind, until,
in a sudden
wind and vanishing
fog, they look up:
not to worship,
but, more, from habit;
the way, once left
home when their men
went to rivet
the thing, they said
morning prayers.
Even on Sunday,
now, of course,
they accept how

the shadow swings
down, leaning
in and away
in elliptic rings
like a sundial.
Or so a high
state official
told them it did,
when they, craning
that broken sky,
sat assembled
there for the long
dedication:
it resembled,
he said, nothing
so much; and laughing
then, said if you
knew where you were
(they laughed too),
and perhaps how far
from the solstice,
you could almost tell
what time it was,
by when the shadow
fell on your house.
Not that the tower
itself would fall,
ever, on such
a quiet meadow
of homes, nor would
the isogonic reaction
affect, even touch,
their elm trees;
the theta conductors
were shielded, at

his personal direction,
he said, so not
to entail any risk
for them, or their families.
A man, then, stood
tall, as if to ask
a first question, but
near him a guard
preserved order.
There was, the speaker
admitted, an odor
caused by the breaker
circuits, but this
was the new power,
in essence, and, as
designed, wouldn't last.
A solar device,
he called it, strong
as the Nation
itself, which, because
of such structures,
would stand until
Kingdom Come.
They were proud there,
then; and still are,
when their children,
or children's children,
home from municipal
lectures, recite,
without prompting,
the smallest detail:
the interval
of each warning light,
and how, just
at dawn, the strange

26

orange glow
on top will go
out, with something
suspended, like
lazing snow
in the morning air;
not much, a flake
here, a flake there,
which dissolves
to a kind of dust
and settles, daily,
around the globular
base. And, daily,
the child who puts up
the flag is assigned,
also, to sweep.
Once every year
they make wreaths
(of jagged cut felt,
shaped like elm leaves)
and lay them here,
between the new sidewalk
and Main Street.
Otherwise, nothing
is changed: home
is the same, talk
still revolves
around the same
people. Government
studies, given
every control,
have proven
this. The report
is unanimous,
to every intent:

there's been neither
famine nor war.
Their original
fear of the fall
is gone, the range
of the shadow
seems less, the weather
more clear. The meadows
are full of new flowers;
stakes are aligned
on most lawns, shaped
like sundials.
Women count hours
still; they repeat
household trials,
and gossip. But
except for
the fool who tried
climbing the tower,
few have died;
most have escaped
the usual town
diseases; misbegotten
children are
fewer, the suicide
rate is down.
Indeed, nothing
is ominous
here, unless
you take stock
of their dreams:
waking, sometimes,
they say, it hangs
over them: not
exactly the tower

itself, but what
they've forgotten,
something above
the tower, like
a dance tune
they can't quite
remember, or name.
They are used to
the circuit breakers
now; they admit
it, even to
Government
census-takers,
who wake them—
women weeping
over their sleeping
men, at dawn—
since only then,
before day
begins, will they
try to show,
without words,
but pointing towards
the tower, that what
they can't name
is, like waking
itself, or making
love, not different,
no, but in spite
of the Government,
yes, not quite
the same.

NEBRASKA, U.S.A.

In this far flat land, far from any home
you might come home to, you stand where distance
has no end. Give or take a blank white farm
in all these square-mapped miles, perspective
is no more than one long narrowing down linear roads
or rows of corn. You know that no directive
could, if given, see you further than a county line,
but only deeper inland then, you'd violate
a kind of boundary for which there is no sign.

Even where plowed contours hold back rain, there is
no height of land to look off from; the crop grows taller
than a man, and there is nothing to imagine but this
green infinity of fodder that's centered where you stand.
Walk on, or in, or think you're walking out: the corn
moves with you and you end where you began. Such land
amazes strangers; immigrants at harvest, blessed
with new security, they settle in the furrowing
of their first view, not knowing where they're lost.

Centered here, how can men hope to know what hail
may thresh them down in June? Big as the sky builds up,
there is no range on which to plot the tallest anvil
cumulus; and when the storm falls out, dead over-
head, there is no channel for the flood. Where winds
twist level, mile on mile, no wonder men take cover
in their cellars. When the high-school sirens sound,
winding their own tornado out across these blank
horizons, there is no place to go but underground.

THE TOTAL CALM

We had, at midnight, flicked the outside light
and watched the first thin spit of snow, a flurried
swirl, as if off some cold edge of heaven
blown with such high force that—where we looked
to see our still bare driveway through the glass,
through floodlit gusts—it seemed the house was **driven**.

Then in a softened wind, we saw the flat
flakes hang, drift up and spin, until we heard
a squall hiss through the oak's stiff leaves, and guessed
that it had settled down to snow. House locked,
we looked out at the last thin spears of grass
bent through the storm whose forecast we had missed.

Before we banked the fire, the lights went out
the way the stars had gone at dusk. With power
lost, we slept downstairs and, waking cold
beside cold ashes, wondered how we'd weathered
sleep to this faint dawn and yet not heard
some rusted town-plow buck the drifted world.

Mute as birds, we faced a flat gray light:
the snow built up against our plate-glass door
like glacial strata, white on white, as if
some soft slow-motion avalanche had gathered
weight behind it, while we slept, and had
at last been loosened from an unknown cliff.

Into the solstice, then, we woke toward silence;
and listening out in hope some winter bird
might sing, we climbed up-attic where the stretch

of snow—a nowhere left to tunnel to, impassable
tough mounds that might be trees, the earth at zero—
lay blanked as far as our two minds could reach.

It might have, at the year's uneasy balance,
melted out and been the other flood;
yet this ungodly cold, these depths that whelm us,
are let down from altitudes impossible
to judge, as if from emptied realms where snow,
unmelting snow, is all that's left to calm us.

IF IT COMES

If it comes
to that, go
to bed late,
so, if you
have to wait
without sleep,
you can see
the luminous
dial, and keep
watch on your
self-winding
pulse. Words bug
the least light,
and full-moon
animals, out
to shuttle
the dark, drag
a trapped leg
through the rose
bed. Last night
was the same:
the same noise,
the slow night-
lock rattle,
and no one
there. Finding
yourself where
bat wings swim
the blank sky,
where owls dive
to echo
your own dark

question, yes,
you must go
to bed late:
so, if for
once, you have
enough warning,
enough to break
out, from what
pass as dreams,
you will wake,
if it comes,
near morning.

NIGHT NOTES ON AN OLD DREAM

Like a seal
in broken sleep,
aware of how
cold the moonlight
lies on salt ice,
I let the sea
work. The floodtide
under my skull,
lugged by the full
March moon, under-
cuts the barrier
shelf, folds back, and
opens a lead
to my forehead.
The moon waves in.
Adrift, and washed
by the equinox,
I let the sea
work. Under me
the shelf calves off;
my sleep ebbs east,
offshore. Sure, for
once, I'm neither
mad nor dead, I
dive awake from
the floe where last
night's snowbirds rise;
and I count them,
white and moonstruck,
climbing, beyond
Orion, to the moon
behind my eyes.

THE OWL

I thought he'd gone, that owl,
to wherever owls winter at.
But no, he's out there still,
hooing the cold, awake
to what small things an owl
can hear under those big fake
horns. My eyes blink shut,
but his are full of the dark,
and see. I saw him once,
at noon, when they wouldn't work,
and he sat sleeping, up
in a deadwood oak, looking more
like a displaced giant moth
than a bird of prey. Except
for his triple talons, which tore
at the branch, or at dreams, while he slept,
he sat unruffled, and aloof.
I tried to stone him off,
but I missed; his dreams were remote,
and swaying, he never woke.
Or say he waited me out.
That was ten days ago,
and I'm still unsure of us both.
By our different lights, we're blind
two ways to our different stake
in these woods. I hear him hoo,
again, and think of the beak
those dove sounds issue from.
I'm frozen, too. I'd sleep
if I could, while he hunts,
but I've got a mind to outlast him.
And this time, but not to cast

stones, I stretch and walk out,
to find what he's hunting for.
Not that I think this first snow
will be full of tracks to identify;
that owl, from whatever tree
he looks down, has only an eye
for what's warm, and shivering
still, with a need to run free.
Awake where my eyes adjust
to the dark, I stand frozen now,
and I begin to see.

II

II

THE LINE

It's not, at sea, like crossing the equator,
not a line you're schooled to navigate—
though fools have run their easting down, Capetown
to Perth, solo, in hope old Neptune
would meet them halfway, with a mermaid,
rum, and some engraved certificate.

The initiation is secret, as Conrad knew.
Crossing at night in the Gulf of Siam,
a man can find himself in stays, unsure
of his first command; yet need no braid,
then or again, to weather whatever mutiny.
Nansen froze his way across, in the *Fram*.

Shackleton crossed in the Scotia Sea,
but he, like Captain Slocum, left no chart
to fix the latitude of his crossing. You
could track the *Spray,* sister her hull,
tack to survive Magellan's straits, and still
not cross. It's not a line you'd know to plot,

though you signed Bowditch as your navigator.
Until you find yourself hove-down, lost,
in masthead seas, and sight it dead abeam,
no other voyage helps define
your bearing on this course; but once you leave
it clear astern, you'll know what you have crossed.

III

VIII

THESE MEN

for M.V.D.

What is man, that mindful of him
in his last act, I let tears blind me?
Scene after scene, his voice
is his sword's, yet when chaste stars illumine
his justice, his choice
is finally to fall from the height his words
must reach. These men remind me.

Not that through their thin mask I name
them, walking on in crossed light, or pray
to a stage that time will revolve.
Too frail to be gods, men who need women
and silence, who love
to be loved, they risk their trial words
to redeem not themselves but the play.

Speaking, they speak cast out of time:
a prince who would break up the dumb-show,
a kingdom-dividing king, a son
at the crossroads; they question how common
it is to be man,
and measured for death by their words'
grave rise, sentence themselves to know.

DEAD MAN'S TALK

Standing, once,
I saw a man
stand tall, his arms
and eyes aimed out
five feet in front
of his feet, his wrists
cocked back, each hand
palm down, as if
he thought to fall.
I thought he'd half
pushed gravity
away; but no,
he dove: his heels
kicked back and up,
flat out on the air—
where, ever since,
I've heard the sound
of his hands, clapped *one-
two-free,* before
he pressed himself,
clown that he
was, to the cold
ground we share.

FIRST DRAFT

for J.W.

Wanting a poem, Jim,
waking blank, I try
to count old oak leaves
rusted in the rain;
I want to stay the wind,
and make my rainy saying
move you as your mind,
at equinox, moves me;
to let you see the leaves,
and how their drift,
outward more than down,
leaves time, for once,
to play at playing God
and trying one right word;
but I hear you, far inland,
speak back to my island:
Time is always left,
there's no last word for love;
there's only this first world,
the poem all poems are part of.

PAINTER

Listen, Ben Shahn,
your hands work good:
I mean the way
you paint hands big
and weight your arms
with what it takes
to earn a wage,
and how your faces
feel the thunder shape
of trains that shake
their dirt backyard;
I mean the way
those coalcars shook
Scott's Run, and how,
on one drawn breath,
you painted: *Look!*

THE DIVE

for M., beginning analysis

You could, of course, see more with a mask,
stay down longer with air tanks, or surface
more surely with fins. But how you dive
will be what you hold up to the sun;
and will measure, better than amphora,
gold, or depth-gauge, where you have been.
Relics are not what you gasp to retrieve,
under such darkening pressures: you surface,
if barely, having recovered your self.

MARIN

Marin
saw how it feels:
the first raw shock
of Labrador current,
the surfacing gasp
at jut of rock,
bent sails, and wedged
trees. He wrote it:
Stonington, Small
Point, and Cape Split,
through a pane so
cracked by the lode-
star sun that he
swam back, blinded,
into himself, to
sign the after-
image: initialed
mountains, ledged
towns (white as
Machias after
the hayrake rain),
sun-splintered
water and written
granite; dark light
unlike what you
ever saw until,
inland, your own
eyes close and, out
of that sea-change,
islands rise thick,
like the rip-tide

paint that, flooding,
tugs at your vitals,
and is more Maine
than Maine.

MAINE

When old cars get retired, they go to Maine.
Thick as cows in backlots off the blacktop,
East of Bucksport, down the washboard
from Penobscot to Castine,
they graze behind frame barns: a Ford
turned tractor, Hudsons chopped to half-ton
trucks, and Chevy panels, jacked up,
tireless, geared to saw a cord of wood.

Old engines never die. Not in Maine,
where men grind valves the way their wives grind axes.
Ring-jobs burned-out down the Turnpike
still make revolutions, turned marine.
If Hardscrabble Hill makes her knock,
Maine rigs the water-jacket salt: a man
can fish forever on converted sixes,
and for his mooring, sink a V-8 block.

When fishing's poor, a man traps what he can.
Even when a one-horse hearse from Bangor fades
away, the body still survives:
painted lobster, baited—off Route 1—
with home preserves and Indian knives,
she'll net a parlor-full of Fords and haul in
transient Cadillacs like crabs. Maine trades
in staying power, not shiftless drives.

BUILDER

A stump of a man, Mace works wood:
a pine block first, whittled and shaped
to a model half-hull. "Now you take
the old *Annie Gott*," he says. He carves
the memory out, pine-chip and spit-
to-windward, lugging full sail, by eye.
A Deer Isle man, he mates and survives
his own stories, gales the old *Annie Gott*
weathered out (". . . and never, by God,
reefed down"); he reaches the grain he hoped
for: he worries the sheerline, the rake
of the stem. His hands never lie.

His woodlot gets cut in November:
bucksaw and double ax. The planks
season, cedar and oak, while he lofts
the lines out: scaling the model up
to full size, beam and deadrise walked out
on the floor of the wharf. He can't read,
or swim, but he floats the wineglass shape
of the stern by unwritten laws. The pot-
belly stove heats up: "You remember
Levi Colson? Off on the Banks,
fogged in tight in a peapod . . ." Talk drifts
downwind, but by April the keel gets laid.

By adze and hatchet, Mace scrolls the shavings
off clean. He sets up transom and stem
like old stories: "Wasn't a vessel could beat
the *Annie*. Stiff? Well, mister . . ." He levels
the keel a last time, and hangs his plumbline
true from the bow. "Once, off Isle au Haut . . ."

Tacking, he looks for a tool, and bevels
the deadwood smooth. "If she was mine,
I'd rig her gaff, like the *Annie*." His shavings
swept, he fires up rib-scraps for steam,
bending hot oak, like the truth itself, to meet
and survive any last Nor'east blow.

By late May she takes shape: he hums when he
pays in the caulking, and jibes back, eying
her lines, as he planes the planked hull.
His wife died last fall. Time is ebbing
under the wharf; a fair tide and a last coat
of gloss on this vessel, he'll launch a yacht.
Her topsides primed, he touches her, rubbing
his gut, to draw the line where she'll float.
As she will, to the last eighth-inch, in any
sea, designed by his winters of lying
hove-to in this shop—with her lee-rail
dry in a gale, like the old *Annie Gott*.

JAKE'S WHARF

Days like this, off Jake's, the August fog
scales up on millpond mornings. Harbor gulls
float quiet as classboats in the leaning tide
(a gray gull rides the spar buoy on one leg
at noon); by four, blown home, they stand parade
on Jake's streaked roof, and summer moors as Sou'west
smoke furls in across the Camden Hills.

Come Labor Day, these weather breeders end:
Jake's brightwork dinghies hauled, the mackerel sky
floods schools of rainsqualls on the wharf; September
tides wash through the boatshed where the wind
backs in Northeast; three driven days the timber
creaks, no boat puts off, and only the fish hawks,
cast from bent fir, fish down the spume-lined Bay.

There is another weather then, a day
swung hard Northwest, when every island spruce
stands sharpened in the wind's cold lens and rises,
like Blue Hill, in arctic clarity;
now lobstermen set traps where each wave blazes
in the splintered sun; upriver, seals
lie ledged across the tidal Bagaduce.

Days after these ebb gray without a thaw.
For some few men the winter sea is farmland
and front yard: off Jake's they drag for scallops,
hand-line cod, and tie up cold where tar
and marline flavor talk that mends the traps.
Time closes in, like snow on cradled yachts,
now people from away have driven inland.

These are the weathers Jake knew to weather out
and wait for, slow in the woodstove warmth of his shop
where, days like this, he used to steam-bend oak,
or bend to plank a skiff, with his weather eye out
for a high March sky. But now, to a snow-swirl wake
of gulls, his lobster boat swings cold at the mooring;
the wharf leans seaward in the ebb-tide chop.

THE ANCHOR

for D. and L.

The wind submerges this house.
Snow, with a whole gale
and an ocean behind it,
surfs into the fir trees
and floods the east window.

Small storms, like minnows
schooled down off the roof,
sound into our sight; our eyes
swim out toward infinity
from this drifting house,

but the Christmas anchor
you gave us holds, hooked deep.
Though a whitecap wind
still spumes the high spruce,
as over Burnt Cove

the night you conned us home
and hung one riding light
for both boats, we lie swung
on the long rode of your giving,
secured for sleep. Afloat

in dissolving spindrift here,
we harbor hope for another
season, with you who weather
your own cold solstice out,
and leave swinging-room

to anchor together, boat-
and-boat; as not to drag now
we turn through white squalls
to each other, and learn
to give love full scope.

THE NARROWS

a prothalamion for K. and A.

Hackmatack, juniper, spruce,
slope back and up from the tidal sluice
of The Narrows, the land half island
and the sea half ledge. Even seals can find
no passage save when the tide is slack.
At half-tide, miniature whirlpools
guard the inner cove; you must choose
your time, and wait, as the sleek seals
do, who come to love the sun,
and surface under a North horizon
spired by spruce and hackmatack.

Where you, at landfall, wait
offshore while the flood begins to make,
bear carefully on the juniper slope
that lifts behind The Narrows. Lie luffed-up,
until, as you feel the helm go loose
in your hand, the tide begins to steer you.
The entrance is blind; you must shape
your drift to the current's choice, clear to
the seals, arrived already, who dive
to find themselves calm in this cove,
ringed by hackmatack and spruce.

Set your hook here, harbored
against the sea, with seals to starboard,
and evergreen shores as your port. Bare
to dip once, indulge the sun, before
—as you must—you finally favor the tide.
Only the cove remains, renewed

by the sea, as you—swung in anchored
sleep between flood and ebb—are renewed
by juniper, spruce, and hackmatack;
and, through The Narrows, bear your luck back
to the old raw weathers of the sea outside.

THE TURNING

It softens now. April snow
sinks melting in the lawn, the swamp
is blurred with promises, the willow
hazed faint green. A month ago

the view was longer. Through the fence,
by a last birch hung with ice-glazed
bittersweet, two cock pheasants
fed, and risked their iridescence.

Faced with snow, and a North wind,
no bird or woodlot animal owns
protective color; nor does a mind
that hunts the contrasts of this land

when its cold distances freeze clear.
It softens now. The frozen rabbit
melts, his fine blood-matted hair
dissolves to mold. The fertile year

revolves toward groundfog after rain,
and where the pheasants fed, raw bloodroot and skunk cabbage blur the line
of fenceposts. No distances define

what's near. Nor yet, in these rich signs
that blend toward spreading camouflage,
grows any sight of the bitter vines
which will choke the birch in soft designs.

THE ROUND

Skunk cabbage, bloodroot,
ginseng, spring beauty,
Dutchman's-breeches,
rue, and betony;

bluets, columbine,
cowslip and bittercress,
heartleaf, anemone,
lupin, arbutus;

bunchberry, merrybells,
Jack-in-the-pulpit,
hepatica, vetch,
and dogtooth violet;

pussy-willow, starwort,
wet-dog trillium,
alumroot, lady's-slipper,
Solomon's-plume;

milkweed, fireweed,
loosestrife and dogbane,
sunbright, buttercup,
thistle, and pipevine;

paintbrush, bunchlily,
chicory, candy-root,
spatterdock, sundew,
touch-me-not;

goldenrod, aster,
burdock and coral-

root, gentian, ragweed,
jumpseed, and sorrel;

upland yellow-eye
and Joe-pye-weed,
bittersweet, sumac,
snow, and frozen seed.

THE ISLANDERS

Winters when we set our traps offshore,
we saw an island further out than ours,
miraged in midday haze, but lifting clear
at dawn, or late flat light, in cliffs that might
have been sheer ice. It seemed, then, so near,

that each man, turning home with his slim catch,
made promises beyond the limits of his gear
and boat. But mornings we cast off to watch
the memory blur as we attempted it,
and set and hauled on ledges we could fetch

and still come home. Summers, when we washed
inshore again, not one of us would say
the island's name, though none at anchor sloshed
the gurry from his deck without one eye
on that magnetic course the ospreys fished.

Winters, then, we knew which way to steer
beyond marked charts, and saw the island, as
first islanders first saw it: who watched it blur
at noon, yet harbored knowing it was real;
and fished, like us, offshore, as if it were.

MATINICUS

68°55′W—43°52′N

Further out than a mainland eye
can see, it lies hull-down in the mind,
an island that you reach for, hazed
in the lightest airs, somewhere offshore
until it lifts across, and off,
the flat blue curve far out: a landfall
wavering more in time than distance.
No compass, no degrees and minutes,
can chart you back, who stand watch first
for No Man's Land, and a reef awash
where the swell breaks white like a whale.
The floodtide sets you, past the bell;
you remember now, and anchor close in,
in the hooked cove where fishhouses shine
in the new-paint sun. The shore is slant
granite slabs, blank windows looking out
from white clapboard, where the catwalks sag
seaward from door to front door; the plank
weathered, like bait tubs, or the thin pier
stilted back to black spruce. The churchspire,
high ashore, might be the landmark
for your bearing here. Or Matinicus Rock,
where (homing on the diaphone
or light) you might come to find puffin
after a two-reef windward beat.
But anchored now, with a lobsterboat
astern, and the whole sea behind you,
you recognize your holding ground
and know what deviation swung
your compass back: set out along

the catwalk windows' opened frames,
Matinicus geraniums,
as for the twenty summers you forgot,
blaze like light buoys, each in a tin-can pot.

PROPELLER

Caged lightly by two-by-fours, rigged flat
on a low-bed trailer, a bronze propeller
sits stranded off Route 1. It almost
fills both lanes: traffic stacks up
behind it; and each car, passing, reflects
its moment of the five blades' pure color.

Honking won't move such a roadblock.
Halfway, here, from its molten state,
far inland, it waits an ocean: still
to be keyed, then swung home, in a river dredged
with old histories of launching and salvage.
Incomplete though it is, and late,

it will get there, somehow. Even
as a huge tourist attraction, it cost
too much to leave as part of civilization's
roadside debris. It's curious, here,
wondering at the magnitude of such work,
to think how finally diminished

the size will seem, in place, and of how
submerged its ultimate function will be.
But even now, as if geared to a far interior
impulse, it churns the flat light: as far
from here its cast will turn against time,
and turn dark, and it will move the sea.

SABLE ISLAND

60°W—43°56′N

You wouldn't want to go there. Sand
is all there is: a graveyard strip
of ships' bones in the North Atlantic;

backbones, deadeyes, ribs, cast up
like the dune itself, by an antic
surf. Cabot chose not to land.

A Portugese pilot first named it,
Santa Cruz, drifting for fish
on the king's orders; it was longer

then, before the unchristly wash
of wind broke up the bar in stranger
shapes than the Cross, which never formed it.

All known charts, by 1546,
marked its luck as Sable, prized
as bad luck, for the centuries

of full-sail trade which civilized
that beach, with skeletons and crosstrees.
Two hundred and fifty known wrecks

ghost it now: Gloucestermen,
British men-o'-war, and Greeks,
Nova Scotiamen, and Vikings.

Henry stranded his Bastille convicts
there, with pardons. A woman with rings
on her fingers, lost there when

the ship *Amelia* sank, with all hands,
had an emerald hacked off her corpse,
by professional wreckers. People have tried

to live there, all right; lighted hopes,
seed, cattle, most of which died.
Ganged horses still churn those sands,

wild as the madmen shipped to asylum,
and burial, there. A Boston parson
petitioned to own it once, but granted

his gift, could find no sane person
to harvest the crop he claimed his stunted
bushes grew, in that private Elysium.

There was a harbor there, years ago.
But where, only God knows, now that
the tides have sanded it, smooth as an eel.

Save for the cumulus hung in mounted
thermals over those flat dunes, still
as fast-ice, you wouldn't know

a landfall was in the offing; not even
close in, if you'd drifted forty hours
in a lifeboat, and woke with the sea making up,

and the first fog lifted. No upraised oars
will get you help here, half swamped by the chop,
and not so much bound to any haven

ahead as running, hull-down in the heavy
troughs, from any last watch kept aloft,
and all false havens astern. Only the loud

surf sounds this shore, patrolled by a raft
of gulls, and buoyed by the anvil cloud.
Half-drowned fishermen, home from Davy

Jones' fleet, tell how the first boy born
to castaways here will be island king.
But no one yet has survived this beachhead

by divine right, or weathered the breaking
tons of sea to couple his hope with dead
myths. The cloud itself might warn

you away. Yet sighting it first from an open
boat, like many who risk the sea,
you have no choice of refuge left.

You might even, tugged in under the lee
of this island, think yourself safe,
and forget its history, or how you happen

to be here. Seen from a mast-step broken
by gales, it looks huge. As it is. No
matter what new disasters to come, you must shape

your course into the breakers as though
it were the whole world, not just a strip
of blown sand you happen to be cast up on.

NOTES

Notes

Almost any word a poet adds to his poems, whether as a fore-
word to a public reading, or as an afterword to a book, is
bound to annoy those literary scientists in his audience who
delight in solving obscure verbal puzzles on a do-it-yourself
basis, and such words will always be suspect in such prosaic
minds as search (with malice aforethought) for confirmation
of their certainty that the poet is, by definition, an unclear
sort of thinker who is only demonstrating his own confusions
in trying to explain them away. Both kinds of readers will, I
suspect, have long since shelved this book in favor of return-
ing to Double-Crostics or The Collected Quatrains of Eustacia
Keats Willingham.

If these island poems are complex, it is because the world
of which they're a part is not simple; if they are anywhere
difficult for certain inland readers, I would like to think that
their difficulty derives from the sometimes specialized language of the sea. If they are obscure, in the sense that they
do not own meaning in their own right and do not relate to
the world or the poems which surround them, they are bad
poems and deserve to be left unread. Notes, at best, can only
provide perspective on the shadowy beach-fire light that a
good poem casts; even then, I realize, they may seem to argue
some wasteland syndrome. But I like to pay my debts when
I can; I want to familiarize inlanders with the hard accuracy
of metaphors native to the coast; and where I am conscious
of the impulse which catalyzed one or another of these poems,
I can only hope that my sense of it may enable the most gen-

erous of readers to experience the poems themselves more
deeply.

The Second Noon: Beyond thanks for marriage and the Book
of Genesis, I am specifically grateful to *The Unquiet Grave* of
Cyril Connolly: "In my religion all believers would stop work
at sundown and have a drink together 'pour chasser la honte
du jour.' This would be taken in remembrance of the first sun-
set when man must have thought the oncoming night would
prove eternal. . . ."

Spit: The phrase "Under-the-Blanket" is part of the journal
which survived Art Moffatt's expedition. I take it to mean
what his context clearly suggests: sex in sub-zero tempera-
tures. Details concerning the government bounty given to the
Chipewyans on the anniversary of their treaty with Canada
are his, as is the structure of the game itself. The import of
the game I extend by my own sense of it.

*Night Notes on an Old Dream: A Functional Glossary of Ice
Terminology* (U.S. Navy Hydrographic Office Publication No.
609), I find, scientifically confirms my maybe racial memory
of "the barrier shelf," leads, and calving floes. Confirmation
of the poem's more lunar instincts may be found, however un-
scientifically, in *The Log from the Sea of Cortez,* as they are
shared by John Steinbeck and E. F. Ricketts: "The prepon-
derantly aquatic symbols of the individual unconscious might
well be indications of a group psyche-memory which is the
foundation of the whole unconscious. . . . Perhaps, next to
that of the sea, the strongest memory in us is that of the moon.
But moon and tide and sea are one. Even now, the tide estab-
lishes measurable, though minute, weight differential. For ex-
ample, the steamship *Majestic* loses about fifteen pounds of its
weight under a full moon (Marmer, *The Tide,* 1926, p. 26).
According to a theory of George Darwin (son of Charles

74

Darwin), in pre-Cambrian times, more than a thousand million years ago, the tides were tremendous; and the weight differential would have been correspondingly large. The moon-pull must have been the most important single environmental factor of littoral animals. Displacement and body weight must then certainly have decreased and increased tremendously with the rotation and phases of the moon, particularly if the orbit was at that time elliptic. . . . Tidal effects are mysterious and dark in the soul, and it may well be noted that even today the effect of the tides is more valid and strong and widespread than is generally supposed."

The Line: "Capetown to Perth" is, for men who risk offshore voyages, one of the world's longest passages without sight of land. To run one's "easting down" is to head east (hopefully downwind) on an established line of latitude. Neptune, by the traditions of the sea, initiates voyagers when they cross the equator for the first time, but "the line" of this poem is closer to Conrad's "The Shadow Line" than to any mid-ocean meridian, and whoever has crossed his own line will have long since sailed beyond the mock-honor of such an "engraved certificate" as might be presented to him in some swimming-pool ceremony on a Caribbean cruise ship.

Conrad's sense of one man's crossing, in the Gulf of Siam, is dramatized in "The Secret Sharer." Standing inshore to permit his alter ego a swimmer's chance at the land which will give him his freedom, the captain of this story deliberately risks his "first command" (and mutiny) as he steers his ship in so dangerously slow a shifting of her course that she barely keeps her maneuverability; she is, then, "in stays."

Fridtjof Nansen, in 1894, deliberately froze his specially designed *Fram* in the Arctic ice, in order to ascertain the drift of the polar ice pack. Sir Ernest Shackleton, on his *Endurance* expedition to the Antarctic, sailed a twenty-two-foot lifeboat

75

some nine hundred miles across the Scotia Sea to South Georgia, in order to provide rescue for those of his crew marooned on Elephant Island.

Joshua Slocum was master of the thirty-six-foot sloop *Spray,* the first solo circumnavigator (1895–1898), and the author of an offshore *Walden* called *Sailing Alone Around the World.* The hull of the *Spray* has been sistered, or duplicated, by many aspirants to Captain Slocum's fame, but none has had (or wanted) to duplicate his miraculous double passage of the Strait of Magellan. Like Melville's Bulkington, the fictional archetype of all men who act on their knowledge that "in landlessness alone resides the highest truth," Slocum was typically reticent about bringing word ashore of where or when he crossed his own line. But in the Strait, if anywhere, when he was "hove down" (with all sail furled) in seas as high as the top of his mast, he surely survived by instincts beyond what he learned from the standard treatise on navigation, Nathaniel Bowditch's *American Practical Navigator.*

These Men: My debt to Mark Van Doren is beyond telling, not least as the unspoken text of his Columbia University course in tragedy and comedy was, surely, Psalms 8:4. My specific references in the third strophe are, of course, to Hamlet, Lear, and Oedipus; the "chaste stars" of line 4 derive from *Othello,* V.ii.2.

Painter: Ben Shahn is, to my seeing, one of the few painters whose hands "work good" as they work well. The painting on which the poem focuses is "Scott's Run, West Virginia," a 1937 work now owned by the Whitney Museum of American Art.

Marin: John Marin was, like Ryder and Homer, one with the sea itself; the greatest of them all when it came to painting

Maine. Small Point, Stonington, and Cape Split were his home ports, as he ventured continually east to seek a further purification of his vision. As Frederick S. Wight suggests in the catalogue of the John Marin Memorial Exhibition (1955), he spoke repeatedly of his paintings as "writings," shaped his mountains into the initial M, and drew rain over such downeast fish-towns as Machias in the form of a dark-pronged hayrake.

Maine: Downeast fishermen, unable to afford stock marine engines for their lobsterboats, often convert Chevrolet engines to marine use, primarily by rigging a salt-water cooling jacket around the six-cylinder block.

Builder: A builder like Mace Eaton, who can't read the small print on a blueprint, makes an art of his craft, in the oldest traditions of the sea. His memory of able boats is generations deep, and he designs new boats by whittling out a half-model of his memory, with the slight variations of deck-curve (sheerline) or bow-angle (stem) that are his native genius. Multiplying the measurements of this model, he lays out (or "lofts") a full-size plan on the uneven floor of his wharf. His tools are his grandfather's, and his craftsmanship is close to instinctual, as is his mysterious ability to draw on a cradled hull the waterline which, inevitably, will mark the precise line where the launched boat will float. Mace sailed the *Annie Gott* as a young man, and has never finished his serial narrative of her virtues, chief of which was her "stiffness," or ability to survive whatever punishment nor'easters, or Mace, might give her.

Jake's Wharf: The Bagaduce is a violently tidal river running in front of what was Jake Dennett's old wharf. It forms part of Castine harbor, from which winter fishermen used to put

77

ashore at Jake's to mend their lobster traps and tar their gear. Jake would, meantime, be firing up his steam box to bend the oak ribs for whatever rowboat he was slowly building in hope of a summer profit.

The Anchor: To "con" is to pilot a boat through a difficult passage. A "riding light" is hung from an anchored boat at night. To give "full scope" to an anchor "rode" (or rope) is, literally, to permit a vessel the easy tether (or "swinging room") which will keep her from dragging onto the rocks.

The Narrows: A tide "begins to make" when it starts to come in. To "bear" on a juniper slope, or wherever, is to establish one's navigational location in reference to a known factor. To "lie luffed up" is to head into the wind, and thus to allow one's sails to flap, or luff, in order to minimize (and ultimately stop) the headway of one's boat. There are many Narrows along any coast of tidal harbors. The Narrows of this poem derive from the Bagaduce River, as it sluices in toward Penobscot, Maine. But Horseshoe Creek on Cape Rosier, or The Basin on Vinalhaven Island, might serve equally as a metaphor.

The Islanders: "Gurry" is the offal of fish. A "magnetic course" is that course figured according to the direction a compass points, in contrast to the True North of the geographical North Pole, or the lines of longitude on a marine chart.

Matinicus: A ship is "hull-down" when only its superstructure, or mast, is showing over the horizon. A diaphone, on which one might aurally set a course comparable to that visibly set on a church spire, is an automatic foghorn. Matinicus Rock, famous for its puffin, is even farther offshore than Matinicus Island, and shortening sail to the extent of a double reef might well be necessary in such seas as surround the Rock. Deviation is that usually metallic local influence on a compass which causes the needle to deviate from magnetic North.

Sable Island: I am indebted to Edward Rowe Snow's various accounts of Sable Island for much of my sense of its history, as well as to Captain Tom Roberts, who ties up at the Boston Fish Pier when he isn't off on the Banks (where dorymen in distress signal their need of help by "upraised oars"). The language of stanzas sixteen and seventeen I have lifted directly from Ishmael's memory of the *Pequod*'s try-works: "Nothing seemed before me but a jet gloom, now and then made ghastly by flashes of redness. Uppermost was the impression that whatever swift, rushing thing I stood on was not so much bound to any haven ahead as rushing from all havens astern."

P.B.
Castine, Maine
1961